AMAZING ANIMALS
OF THE WORLD ①

Volume 5

Hyena, Brown — Mantis, Praying

GROLIER

an imprint of

■SCHOLASTIC

Scholastic Library Publishing

www.scholastic.com/librarypublishing

First published 2008 by Grolier, an imprint of Scholastic Inc.

© 2008 Scholastic Inc.

For information address the publisher: Grolier, Scholastic Library Publishing
90 Old Sherman Turnpike
Danbury, CT 06816

Printed and bound in the U.S.A.

Library of Congress Cataloging-in-Publication Data
Amazing animals of the world 1.
v. cm.
Contents: v. 1. Aardvark-bobcat — v. 2. Bobolink-cottonmouth — v. 3. Coyote-fish, Siamese fighting — v. 4. Fisher-hummingbird, ruby-throated — v. 5. Hyena, brown-mantis, praying — v. 6. Marmoset, common-owl, great horned — v. 7. Owl, pygmy-robin, American — v. 8. Sailfin, giant-spider, black widow — v. 9. Spider, garden-turtle, common musk — v. 10. Turtle, green sea-zebrafish.
Includes bibliographical references and index.
ISBN 0-7172-6225-1; 978-0-7172-6225-0 (set : alk. Paper) - ISBN 0-7172-6226-X; 978-0-7172-6226-7 (v. 1 : alk. paper) - ISBN 0-7172-6227-8; 978-0-7172-6227-4 (v. 2 : alk. paper) - ISBN 0-7172-6228-6; 978-0-7172-6228-1 (v. 3 : alk. paper) - ISBN 0-7172-6229-4; 978-7172-6229-8 (v. 4 : alk. paper) - ISBN 0-7172-6230-8; 978-7172-6230-4 (v. 5 : alk. paper) - ISBN 0-7172-6231-6; 978-0-7172-6231-1 (v. 6 : alk. paper) - ISBN 0-7172-6232-4; 978-0-7172-6232-8 (v. 7 : alk. paper) - ISBN 0-7172-6233-2; 978-0-7172-6233-5 (v. 8 : alk. paper) - ISBN 0-7172-6234-0; 978-0-7172-6234-2 (v. 9 : alk. paper) - ISBN 0-7172-6235-9; 978-0-7172-6235-9 (v. 10 : alk. paper)
1. Animals—Encyclopedias, Juvenile. I. Grolier Incorporated. II. Title: Amazing animals of the world one.
QL49.A453 2007
590.3—dc22

2007012982

About This Set

Amazing Animals of the World 1 brings you pictures of 400 exciting creatures, and important information about how and where they live.

Each page shows just one species, or individual type, of animal. They all fall into seven main categories, or groups, of animals (classes and phylums scientifically) identified on each page with an icon (picture)—amphibians, arthropods, birds, fish, mammals, other invertebrates, and reptiles. Short explanations of what these group names mean, and other terms used commonly in the set, appear in the Glossary.

Scientists use all kinds of groupings to help them sort out the thousands of types of animals that exist today and once wandered the earth (extinct species). *Kingdoms*, *classes*, *phylums*, *genus*, and *species* are among the key words here that are also explained in the Glossary.

Where animals live is important to know as well. Each of the species in this set lives in a particular place in the world, which you can see outlined on the map on each page. And in those places, the animals tend to favor a particular habitat—an environment the animal finds suitable for life—with food, shelter, and safety from predators that might eat it. There they also find ways to coexist with other animals in the area that might eat somewhat different food, use different homes, and so on.

Each of the main habitats is named on the page and given an icon, or picture, to help you envision it. The habitat names are further defined in the Glossary.

As well as being part of groups like species, animals fall into other categories that help us understand their lives or behavior. You will find these categories in the Glossary, where you will learn about carnivores, herbivores, and other types of animals.

And there is more information you might want about an animal—its size, diet, where it lives, and how it carries on its species—the way it creates its young. All these facts and more appear in the data boxes at the top of each page.

Finally, the set is arranged alphabetically by the most common name of the species. That puts most beetles, for example, together in a group so you can compare them easily.

But some animals' names are not so common, and they don't appear near others like them. For instance, the chamois is a kind of goat or antelope. To find animals that are similar—or to locate any species—look in the Index at the end of each book in the set. It lists all animals by their various names (you will find the Giant South American River Turtle under Turtle, Giant South American River, and also under its other name—Arrau). And you will find all birds, fish, and so on gathered under their broader groupings.

Similarly, smaller like groups appear in the Set Index as well—butterflies include swallowtails and blues, for example.

Table of Contents
Volume 5

Glossary

Amphibians—species usually born from eggs in water or wet places, which change (metamorphose) into land animals. Frogs and salamanders are typical. They breathe through their skin mainly and have no scales.

Arctic and Antarctic—icy, cold, dry areas at the ends of the globe that lack trees but are home to small plants that grow in thawed areas (tundra). Penguins and seals are common inhabitants.

Arthropods—animals with segmented bodies, hard outer skin, and jointed legs, such as spiders and crabs.

Birds—born from eggs, these creatures have wings and often can fly. Eagles, pigeons, and penguins are all birds, though penguins cannot fly through the air.

Carnivores—they are animals that eat other animals. Many species do eat each other sometimes, and a few eat dead animals. Lions kill their prey and eat it, while vultures clean up dead bodies of animals.

Cities, Towns, and Farms—places where people live and have built or used the land and share it with many species. Sometimes these animals live in human homes or just nearby.

Class—part, or division, of a phylum.

Deserts—dry, usually warm areas where animals often are more active on cooler nights or near water sources. Owls, scorpions, and jack rabbits are common in American deserts.

Endangered—some animals in this set are marked as endangered because it is possible they will become extinct soon.

Extinct—these species have died out completely for whatever reason.

Family—part of an order.

Fish—water animals (aquatic) that typically are born from eggs and breathe through gills. Trout and eels are fish, though whales and dolphins are not (they are mammals).

Forests and Mountains—places where evergreen (coniferous) and leaf-shedding (deciduous) trees are common, or that rise in elevation to make cool, separate habitats. Rain forests are different (see below).

Freshwater—lakes, rivers, and the like carry fresh water (unlike Oceans and Shores, where the water is salty). Fish and birds abound, as do insects, frogs, and mammals.

Genus—part of a family.

Grasslands—habitats with few trees and light rainfall. Grasslands often lie between forests and deserts, and they are home to birds, coyotes, antelope, and snakes, as well as many other kinds of animals.

Herbivores—these animals eat mainly plants. Typical are hoofed animals (ungulates) that are common on grasslands, such as antelope or deer. Domestic (nonwild) ones are cows and horses.

Hibernators—species that live in harsh areas with very cold winters slow down their functions then become inactive or dormant.

Invertebrates—animals that lack backbones or internal skeletons. Many, such as insects and shrimp, have hard outer coverings. Clams and worms are also invertebrates.

Kingdom—the largest division of species. All living things are classified in one of the five kingdoms: animals, plants, fungi, protists, and monerans.

Mammals—these creatures usually bear live young and feed them on milk from the mother. A few lay eggs (monotremes like the platypus) or nurse young in a pouch (marsupials like opossums and kangaroos).

Migrators—some species spend different seasons in different places, moving to where more food, warmth, or safety can be found. Birds often do this, sometimes over long distances, but other types of animals also move seasonally, including fish and mammals.

Oceans and Shores—seawater is salty, often deep, and huge. In it live many fish, invertebrates, and some mammals, such as whales and dolphins. On the shore, birds and other creatures often gather.

Order—part of a class.

Phylum—part of a kingdom.

Rain forests—here huge trees grow among many other plants helped by the warm, wet environment. Thousands of species of animals also live in these rich habitats.

Reptiles—these species have scales, have lungs to breathe, and lay eggs or give birth to live young. Dinosaurs are thought to have been reptiles, while today the class includes turtles, snakes, lizards, and crocodiles.

Scientific Name—the genus and species name of a creature in Latin. For instance, *Canis lupus* is the wolf. Scientific names avoid the confusion possible with common names in any one language or across languages.

Species—a group of the same type of living thing. Part of an order.

Subspecies—a variety but quite similar part of a species.

Territorial—many animals mark out and defend a patch of ground as their home area. Birds and mammals may call very small or very large spots their territories.

Vertebrates—animals with backbones and skeletons under their skins.

Brown Hyena
Hyaena brunnea

Length of the Body: 3½ to 4½ feet
Length of the Tail: 8 to 10 inches
Weight: about 88 pounds
Diet: dead animals, small antelope, fish, and fruits

Number of Young: 1 to 5
Home: southern Africa
Order: carnivores
Family: aardwolves and hyenas

 Grasslands

 Mammals

© MARTIN HARVEY / PETER ARNOLD, INC.

Endangered Animals

Brown hyenas have loving but unusual families. Their family groups are often large and may include several pregnant and nursing females. Usually the clan shares a cave, where all the adults take turns caring for the pups. If the pups are nursing, they are free to get milk from any available mother. When they are about three months old, young brown hyenas learn to eat meat. The pups will not leave the safety of the cave until they are nearly a year old.

Despite their social family life, brown hyenas do not hunt in packs. They prefer to prowl alone, usually in the dark of night. A solitary brown hyena may travel as far as 30 miles before it returns home the next morning. If the night has been successful, the hyena will bring meat for the pups, as well as for any sick or injured adults that remained behind. Brown hyenas also eat juicy fruits such as melons to quench their thirst. Because they live in an arid habitat, brown hyenas must get water wherever they can.

The brown hyena's range, which may have always been small, overlaps with some of the most populated areas of Africa. These hyenas are often seen hunting for fish and crabs along South African beaches. This habit has earned them the name *strand wolves*. Unfortunately, the same beaches where brown hyenas once roamed free are now full of tourist resorts and homes. Such human crowding has pushed the rare brown hyena to the edge of extinction.

Laughing Hyena
Crocuta crocuta

Length: 4 to 6 feet
Length of the Tail: 8 to 10 inches
Weight: 90 to 140 pounds
Diet: dead animals, young antelope and other mammals, and fruits

Number of Young: usually 2
Home: central and southern Africa
Order: carnivores
Family: aardwolves and hyenas

  Grasslands

Mammals

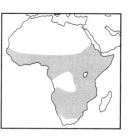

© ARTHUR GLOOR / ANIMALS ANIMALS / EARTH SCENES

The nighttime silence of the African savanna is pierced by a screaming laugh. It is an eerie sound. Natives can tell you that no human is making the noise. It's a laughing hyena. The hyena makes this weird sound for one of two reasons. It is frightened, or it is looking for a mate. At other times the laughing hyena howls. It is a low sound that gradually rises to a high-pitched scream.

This mammal is also called the spotted hyena. This is because of the dark spots scattered over its grayish yellow coat. The pattern of spots changes as the hyena matures. Newborns have a dark brown coat. After about two months, the spotted pattern begins to appear. First it appears on the head and then on the body. As the hyena ages, the spots begin to disappear. Very old hyenas have almost no spots.

The jaws and teeth of laughing hyenas are very powerful. They are strong enough to crush bones. Hyenas prey on various mammals. But they also scavenge. In fact, most of their diet consists of dead animals (carrion). These are often the remains of animals killed by lions. How do you suppose they find the carrion? It might be their sharp sense of smell. Or they may watch the vultures. When the birds descend, hyenas will race to the spot. They steal the rotting meat right from under the vultures' beaks.

Laughing hyenas are active mainly at night. They rest during the day. They do this in dens among rocks or in thick brush. Hyenas live alone or in pairs. Sometimes they even live in small groups.

Alpine Ibex
Capra ibex

Length: 4½ to 5½ feet (male);
2½ to 4 feet (female)
Weight: 150 to 260 pounds
(male); 85 to 110 pounds
(female)
Diet: grasses and herbs
Number of Young: 1

Home: European Alps
Order: even-toed hoofed
mammals
Family: antelope, bison,
buffalo, cattle, goats, and
sheep

 Forests and Mountains

 Mammals

The alpine ibex is recognized by its dramatic, saber-shaped horns. Buck ibex (males) grow massive horns. They can be up to 3 feet long and curl back over their head. During mating season bucks duel by smashing their horns together, head-on. The crashing noise echoes through the Alps, where they live. The horns of does (females) are just over a foot long. They are pointed and straight. The females use them to chase foxes away from their young.

Alpine ibex are excellent jumpers and climbers. The inside surfaces of their hooves are soft. The outside edges are hard. This helps the animal get a sure foothold on rock ledges. Ibex can even climb up vertical rock crevices. They do so by bouncing from one side of the crevice to the other. They use their powerful legs to kick off.

Other than during the winter mating season, male alpine ibex live together in all-male herds. The does and young, called kids, gather in their own groups. The young ibex are playful. They delight in making daring leaps. And they often chase one another along high, narrow cliff ledges.

The alpine ibex was once overhunted. Its horns were mounted as trophies. And its body parts were used in folk medicines. As a result, the ibex population has been greatly reduced. The largest group now lives in a national park in the Italian Alps.

Scarlet Ibis
Eudocimus ruber

Length: 21 to 25 inches
Weight: 18 to 26 ounces
Diet: insects, small fish, and freshwater crustaceans
Number of Eggs: 2 or 3

Home: eastern South America
Order: auks, herons, and relatives
Family: ibises, spoonbills

 Freshwater

 Birds

© MIKE LANE / WWI / PETER ARNOLD, INC.

This bird is famous for its striking plumage. But the scarlet ibis begins life with a decidedly lackluster look. Young birds are dull brown with just a touch of red on the belly and the top of the wings. Not until the ibis reaches sexual maturity does it develop its full color. This happens when it is about two years old. Then the adult males and females grow bright red feathers with distinctive black patches on their wing tips.

Each mated ibis pair defends a small territory within a larger colony. Typically their colonies are in large swamps. They are often on islands with mangrove trees and other marshland plants. The male delivers nest-building materials to his mate. She weaves them into an intricate basket. And she lays her eggs between March and May. The chicks hatch in about three weeks. Soon after hatching, the young birds mingle with the other ibis in the colony. Their protective parents hover overhead like a gorgeous red canopy.

The naturalist P. Allen once wrote, "The living beauty of the scarlet ibis is an enrichment of every country it inhabits." Unfortunately, hunters have killed off many of these birds because native people consider their meat delicious. Scarlet ibis are now protected by law. Today wildlife preserves contain several large, protected scarlet-ibis colonies. The Caroni Sanctuary on the island of Trinidad is one such preserve.

Desert Iguana
Dipsosaurus dorsalis

Length: 10 to 16 inches
Diet: plants, fruits, insects, other arthropods, and carrion
Method of Reproduction: egg layer

Home: southwestern United States and northern Mexico
Order: scaled reptiles
Family: iguanas

  Deserts

Reptiles

© K. H. SWITAK / PHOTO RESEARCHERS

The desert iguana is a desert lizard. It has the highest range of body temperature of that group. Its body temperature peaks as high as 115°F. But that happens only on particularly hot afternoons. The desert iguana is a reptile. It cannot regulate its body temperature internally. Thus, the desert iguana avoids the chill of night and early morning. Unlike most desert creatures, it thrives on heat. It leaves its shelter only when the sun is high in the sky.

The desert iguana is found in sections of the southwestern United States. It also lives in nearby Mexico and favors sandy and rocky areas. It is also known as the desert crested lizard. The creature has a body shaped like a cylinder. It is covered with scales. The iguana is grayish brown. It has an extremely long tail. During the mating season its body changes color. Pinkish or buff areas appear on the stomach of both sexes. The female lays her eggs in the same spot each year. She abandons them soon after. Each iguana feeds in its own particular territory. The desert iguana's main food is plants. It does, however, eat insects and the flesh of dead animals.

The desert iguana is alert yet timid. When frightened, it runs noisily on its hind legs. It can reach speeds of 15 miles per hour. It then seeks shelter in a bush. It may also hide in a hole in the ground. Humans and domestic animals are its worst enemies. It is also prey to hawks and snakes.

Green Iguana
Iguana iguana

Length: up to 6½ feet
Diet: plant matter and insects
Number of Eggs: 20 to 70
Home: Central America and South America

Order: scaled reptiles
Family: iguanas

  Forests and Mountains

Reptiles

© JOE MCDONALD / CORBIS

In a fight between a green iguana and a dog, the dog often loses. This is because of the iguana's not-so-secret weapon—a strong, muscular tail that it whips at its attacker. A well-placed strike of the tail causes enough pain to convince the attacker to look elsewhere for a meal. The iguana may also try to bite its predator with its sharp teeth and powerful jaws. Unfortunately, such weapons do little to protect green iguanas from people who hunt and eat iguanas and their eggs.

Running the length of the green iguana's back is a crest of large scales. On a male the crest may reach up to 3 inches. The green iguana also has a fold of loose skin, called a dewlap, hanging under its neck. As with the crest, the dewlap is larger in the male than in the female.

The green iguana prefers to live in treetops in tropical and subtropical forests. Its well-developed claws are useful in climbing. It often seeks to live near water. There it can take advantage of its excellent swimming ability to escape enemies. When threatened, the green iguana dives below the surface and swims underwater to a nearby band. Some green iguanas live in shrubby coastal regions, where there is a dry season and a rainy season. During the rainy season, plants grow rapidly and food is plentiful. The iguana stores large quantities of fat in its body. This fat helps it survive through the dry season, when food is scarcer.

Impala
Aepyceros melampus

Length: 4 to 5 feet
Height: 3¾ to 4¾ feet (male); 2¼ to 3 feet (female)
Weight: 117 to 165 pounds (male); 88 to 120 pounds (female)
Diet: leaves and grasses
Number of Young: 1

Home: southern and eastern Africa
Order: even-toed hoofed mammals
Family: antelope, bison, buffalo, cattle, goats, and sheep

 Grasslands

 Mammals

© O. ALAMANY & E. VICENS / CORBIS

This antelope of southern and eastern Africa is adapted to racing and jumping. When attacked by lions, leopards, or even humans, it runs away, zigzagging. And it leaps 25 feet, 15 feet, and 30 feet in quick succession. This escape technique makes it difficult to hunt. Moreover, it lives in the wooded savanna. Hunting is very difficult there.

When impalas leap, you can see small black tufts of hair on their rear legs. These tufts cover glands that spread an odor on the ground wherever the impala travels. The smell is a signal that helps the members of the herd find one another when separated.

In the dry season, impalas gather near water in herds. These herds can have as many as 100 animals. But when the rainy season comes, the females and the young get together in herds of 10 to 100 animals. They are led by one male. Other single males form groups of about 60 head. Members of these groups then fight males who head the female and young herds. Two males confront each other and bellow, digging the ground with their horns. Then they push at each other head-to-head, with their horns locked tightly. The winner claims the females. About six or seven months after mating, the female gives birth to a single offspring.

The impala has been hunted extensively. But it is not in danger of disappearing. This animal is protected in African game parks and reserves.

Golden Jackal
Canis aureus

Length: 26 to 30 inches
Length of the Tail: up to 10 inches
Weight: up to 25 pounds
Diet: mainly rodents and birds
Number of Young: usually 4 or 5

Home: Europe, Asia, and Africa
Order: carnivores
Family: coyotes, dogs, foxes, jackals, and wolves

 Grasslands

 Mammals

© HELLIO & VAN INGEN / NHPA / PHOTO RESEARCHERS

Jackals eat almost anything. They chase and catch small mammals, ground birds, reptiles, frogs, fish, and insects. They eat berries and other fruits. They feed on carrion (dead animals), too, including the remains of kills made by lions and other predators. Golden jackals often locate their next meal by watching a vulture, a fellow carrion eater, circling high in the sky. When jackals see a vulture swoop down to feed, they run up to join it at the feast.

Golden jackals live in a variety of habitats in Europe, Asia, and Africa. They are found in hilly areas, on open plains, among bushes at the edge of rivers, and in semidesert regions. They are common near farms, where they will grab chickens and other small domestic animals. They are also found near villages, where they will scavenge at night, feeding on garbage and even human corpses. It's not surprising that many people dislike these creatures!

Golden jackals usually live in small family groups consisting of an adult male, his mate, and their young. The cubs are born in a den, often dug under the roots of a tree or built in an abandoned burrow made by a porcupine or other animal. Both parents care for the cubs. The mother nurses them until they are about three months old and ready to eat solid food.

Jaguar
Panthera onca

Length: 6 feet (male); 5 feet (female)

Weight: 200 to 250 pounds

Diet: small animals, such as deer, peccaries, agoutis, and capybara

Number of Young: 2 or 3

Home: South and Central America to Mexico

Order: carnivores

Family: cats

  Forests and Mountains

Mammals

 Endangered Animals

© KENNAN WARD / CORBIS

The largest meat-eating animal in South America is the jaguar. This big cat is difficult to observe. Scientists know little about its habits. They do know that it usually lives at the edge of the forest. The jaguar hides in tall grass. It is a good climber and excellent swimmer. It can cross the large rivers that pass through the Amazon forest. The forests where they live are shrinking. Many have been cut or burned in recent years. People hunted the cat for its beautiful fur. As a result, it is now endangered and is being protected.

The jaguar has more than one hunting technique. It will chase a herd until one animal tires out and falls behind. The jaguar also hunts by stalking its prey. It is a powerful animal. It can kill a cow or a horse and drag it dozens of yards. It eats a variety of foods. These include capybaras (large rodents) and peccaries (similar to wild pigs). They will even eat monkeys and crocodiles. The jaguar also eats fish. How does it catch fish? It sits on a branch over the water. There it waits for a fish to swim by. Then it grabs it out of the water with its powerful jaws.

A jaguar fiercely defends its territory. It also defends its prey once it has killed it. That is why it sometimes attacks humans who come too close. Except for humans, the jaguar has no enemies. Jaguars generally mate in the fall. Young are born only every other year. They start to eat meat when they are seven weeks old. The cubs stay with their mother for two years. They become adults when they are three or four.

Blue Jay
Cyanocitta cristata

Length: 12 inches
Diet: insects, seeds, nuts, and eggs of other species
Number of Eggs: 3 to 7
Home: east of Rocky Mountains from southern Canada to Gulf of Mexico

Order: perching birds
Family: crows, jays

 Cities, Towns, and Farms

 Birds

© RON AUSTING / FRANK LANE PICTURE AGENCY / CORBIS

The blue jay does not have a good reputation among bird lovers. Indeed, it has many bad habits. Blue jays hog bird feeders and chase away smaller birds. And blue jays imitate the cry of the red-shouldered hawk. They do this so well, in fact, that little birds flee to avoid attack. They leave their nests unprotected. The blue jay then invades the nests. It sucks out the contents of the eggs or eats the chicks.

Fortunately, the blue jay is not all bad. It has brilliant blue feathers, a white underside, and a black-and-white tail. These often add a flash of color to snowy winter days, when most other birds have fled south. Blue jays bury many seeds and acorns that they never retrieve. In this way, blue jays help the environment by planting trees.

Blue jays like trees. They build nests that are bulky but compact. They use twigs, moss, paper, and rags cemented together with mud. In the north, blue jays lay eggs once a year. In the south they lay eggs two or three times. There are usually four to five eggs. But occasionally there are as many as seven. They are warmed almost always by the female. The male, meanwhile, provides food for the female. The eggs hatch after 16 to 18 days. The young jays are fed by both parents. They begin to fly within three weeks of hatching. Some blue jays migrate in loose flocks. Others seem to remain in the same area all year.

Moon Jellyfish
Aurelia aurita

Length: up to 3 inches
Width: up to 16 inches
Diet: protozoans, snail larvae, and other tiny animals
Methods of Reproduction: egg laying and budding

Home: tropical and temperate oceans and seas throughout the world
Order: flag mouth jellyfishes
Family: moon jellies and relatives

 Oceans and Shores

 Other Invertebrates

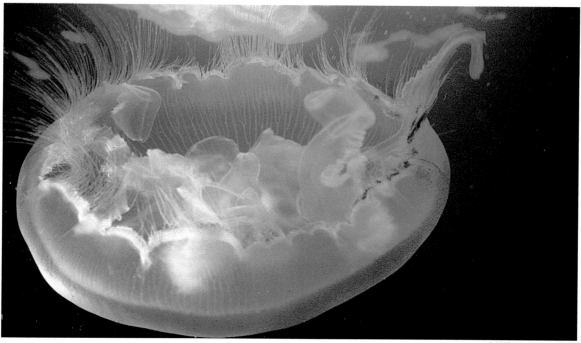

© STEPHEN FRINK / CORBIS

The moon jellyfish has a whitish body shaped like an umbrella. Its body is shallow and saucer like. On the body's rim are hundreds of short tentacles that look like a fringe. The jellyfish swims slowly. As it does it alternately relaxes and contracts its body. When the animal relaxes its body, water enters the central cavity on the underside. When the body is contracted, water is forced out of the cavity. This pushes the animal in the opposite direction.

During high tides and after storms, moon jellyfish may be washed up onto beaches. They are not as poisonous as many other kinds of jellyfish. But their sting can cause a slight rash. The moon jellyfish is not a fish. It is a swimming marine animal. These meat-eating creatures feed on fish and other animals. They catch their prey with the stinging capsules on their tentacles.

The moon jellyfish passes through four stages in its life cycle. These are egg, larva, polyp, and medusa. A fertilized egg develops into a tiny larva. The larva is covered with hairlike fringes. It uses these to swim about in the sea. After a while the larva develops into a polyp with long tentacles. As the polyp eats and grows, it buds off other polyps like itself. Eventually a polyp loses its tentacles and grows longer. It develops a series of horizontal indentations. These make the creature look like a stack of saucers. The saucers separate and swim away as medusae. They gradually grow into adult jellyfish.

Eastern Grey Kangaroo
Macropus giganteus

Length: up to 8 feet, including 3-foot tail
Height: up to 6 feet
Weight: up to 200 pounds
Diet: grasses and other plant matter

Number of Young: 1
Home: eastern Australia
Order: marsupials
Family: kangaroos, wallabies

 Forests and Mountains

 Mammals

© STAFFAN WIDSTRAND / CORBIS

The eastern grey kangaroo is a large marsupial. It has soft fur that is gray on top and white on the belly. As you might suspect, this creature lives in eastern Australia. It is usually found in forests, woodlands, and open fields. The kangaroo is commonly found in groups called mobs. During the day, the mob rests in the shade. The kangaroos begin to move after the sun goes down. Then they forage for food and will feed until early morning.

The eastern grey kangaroo is a vegetarian. It eats only grasses and other small plants. It does so in one of two ways. The kangaroo can graze from the ground like cattle. It can also pick up the vegetation with its front feet and carry the food to its mouth. What happens when a kangaroo is frightened or disturbed? It straightens up and leaps off on its powerful back legs. It may leap 40 feet at a bound. It uses its massive tail as a balance.

Kangaroos give birth at a very early stage of development. A pregnancy lasts only five weeks. At birth an eastern grey kangaroo is less than 1 inch in length. The kangaroo is blind and has no fur when it is born. Its back legs and tail are only tiny buds. The front legs, however, have large, clawed feet. It uses these feet to crawl up its mother's belly to her pouch. The baby is called a joey. Once the joey is in the pouch, it fastens onto a nipple with its mouth. It remains in the pouch for about 11 months. The kangaroo has the longest pouch time of any marsupial.

Red Kangaroo
Macropus rufus

Length: 4¼ to 6½ feet (male);
  3 to 4 feet (female)
Weight: 50 to 200 pounds
Diet: grasses and leaves

Number of Young: 1
Home: Australia
Order: marsupials
Family: kangaroos, wallabies

 Grasslands

 Mammals

© MARTIN HARVEY / CORBIS

The red kangaroo's front legs are very short. Yet its hind legs are long and powerful. When it stands straight on its hind legs, the kangaroo is taller than a human being! It can move forward in great leaps. When it jumps, it uses its tail as a balance. It can reach a speed of 30 miles per hour. And it can cover more than 30 feet with each bound.

The female can give birth in all seasons. The newborn weighs only a few ounces. It is blind, hairless, and not completely formed. But its front paws already have claws. It uses these to crawl along its mother's fur into the pouch. Once inside, it stays there until its growth is complete. This usually takes eight months. It then weighs about nine pounds. It will spend four more months beside its mother. It will occasionally nurse. It nurses even if there is a newborn inside the pouch.

The red kangaroo lives on the hot, dry plains of central Australia. It is the most common large animal there. It eats short, dry grasses and other vegetation. It lives in groups of 6 to 12. An older male acts as the leader. During the day kangaroos rest. They like resting at the foot of a tree or a rock. At night they go out to look for food and drink. Not long ago, they were widely hunted for their meat. It was used for cat food and dog food. They are not protected by law. The kangaroo is Australia's national animal.

Kingfisher
Alcedo atthis

Length: 6 inches
Weight: 1¼ ounces
Diet: fish, insects, worms, and mollusks
Number of Eggs: usually 6 or 7

Home: Europe, Asia, and North Africa
Order: kingfishers, rollers
Family: kingfishers

 Freshwater

 Birds

© JAMIE HARRON; PAPILLO / CORBIS

A kingfisher is poised quietly on a branch above a lake or river, intently studying the water. Suddenly it shoots down into the water and emerges seconds later with a small fish trapped in its beak. Back on the branch, the kingfisher quickly swallows its prize headfirst.

The colorful kingfisher is well built for this type of aerial fishing assault. It is a chunky bird with a short tail and neck, a large head, and a very long and pointed bill. Its plumage is bright blue and green.

Many kingfishers live near fish hatcheries. Most people who operate hatcheries welcome the presence of kingfishers. These birds generally eat the smaller and weaker fish—those that would not sell well at markets. However, in China, people protect their fishponds from hungry kingfishers by covering the ponds with netting.

To make a nest for its young, the female kingfisher digs a hole in soft soil near the banks of rivers and lakes. She removes dirt with her beak and feet until she has created a long tunnel. The kingfisher then lays her eggs at the end of this tunnel. Both parents incubate the eggs for about three weeks and raise the young birds. The young kingfishers dine on regurgitated (thrown-up) pellets of fish that their parents bring them. After about 25 days, the young birds leave the shelter and security of the nest.

Common Kingsnake
Lampropeltis getula

Length: 3 to 6 feet
Diameter: 1 inch
Diet: small reptiles, mammals, and birds
Number of Eggs: 6–12

Home: United States and northern Mexico
Order: scaled reptiles
Family: colubrids, typical snakes

 Forests and Mountains

 Reptiles

© DAVID A. NORTHCOTT / CORBIS

Many a young snake lover has had a common kingsnake as one of his or her first terrarium pets. Though no snake will choose to live in captivity, the kingsnake doesn't seem to mind terribly. It isn't venomous and seldom bites. When someone grabs a kingsnake, it will try to wriggle away. A kingsnake is easy to feed, provided its owner has a ready supply of ordinary mice and small snakes.

Common kingsnakes are abundant from California to New Jersey in environments as varied as prairies, coastal pine forests, marshes, and dry mountains. Because the kingsnake is so widespread, it has evolved into many separate groups known as subspecies. Most subspecies are found in different areas and have different markings.

The groups are not separate species because they could still breed with one another.

The kingsnake is unusual in that some subspecies have two or more dissimilar forms *within* the group. For example, one subspecies found in California comes in two forms: one is black or dark brown with many white rings circling its body; the other has a single white line running from its head to its tail. Biologists say that the kingsnake benefits from having different forms. It may be that the snake's predators have a mental picture of what their food looks like. When such a predator sees another type of kingsnake, it may not recognize it as food and thus leave the unfamiliar-looking creature in peace.

Koala
Phascolarctos cinereus

Length: 24 to 33 inches
Weight: 11 to 26 pounds
Diet: eucalyptus leaves
Number of Young: 1 or 2

Home: southeastern Australia
Order: marsupials
Family: koalas

 Forests and Mountains

Mammals

© B.S.P.I. / CORBIS

There is a strange little animal that lives in the eucalyptus forests of Australia. It is the koala. It must live near eucalyptus trees. Its leaves are this animal's only food. In spite of this, its diet is hardly simple. It eats the leaves of about a dozen different kinds of eucalyptus trees. But the eucalyptus sometimes has poison in its leaves. So the koalas must be careful to avoid them at those times.

Koalas smell like cough drops. Eucalyptus is often used in making cough drops. An adult koala eats two to three pounds of leaves a day. Eucalyptus is a very tough, strong-flavored plant that is hard to digest. To help with digestion the koala has six more feet of intestines than other marsupials. On rare occasions the koala will come down to the ground to change trees. It

then eats some dirt and stones. They help it to digest the leaves. The koala is an excellent climber. It has powerful feet with pointed claws. It uses them to climb up the smoothest tree trunks. If an animal comes into its territory, the koala lets out harsh grating noises. It sounds like a saw cutting wood. It never leaves the trees to get water. It gets enough from the leaves. The name *koala* comes from a native Australian word meaning "no water."

The female usually gives birth to only one pup at a time. The pink baby koala is born without hair. It grows while staying protected in its mother's pouch. It is there for up to 7 months. Then it climbs out and clings to her back. It leaves her when it is about 11 months old.

Kookaburra
Dacelo novaeguineae

Length: 16 to 18 inches
Weight: 14 ounces
Diet: insects, reptiles, and small mammals
Number of Eggs: 2 to 4

Home: eastern and southern Australia and Tasmania
Order: kingfishers, rollers
Family: kingfishers

 Forests and Mountains

 Birds

© MICHAEL MACONACHIE / PAPILIO / CORBIS

Kookaburras are among the noisiest creatures found in Australia. They often are heard even if they aren't seen. People sometimes call them the bushman's clock. This is because flocks of kookaburras typically utter their loud, eerie cries at dawn and dusk. The early morning noise awakens people. It tells them it's time to get out of bed. Another local name for the kookaburra is the laughing jackass. This name arose because its call sounds somewhat like the braying—or "laughing"—of a donkey.

The kookaburra is the largest member of the kingfisher family. Like other kingfishers, it has a rather large head, a short neck, a chunky body, and short legs. Unlike most members of the family, it usually does not eat fish. The kookaburra feeds mainly on large insects and crabs. It also eats small reptiles and mammals. It vigorously attacks its prey with its large, powerful bill. Farmers like this bird because it catches mice, rats, and other pests.

Kookaburras nest during the spring. The female lays her eggs in a tree hole or in a termite nest. Both parents take turns sitting on the eggs. They incubate them for about 25 days. The baby birds are born without feathers and remain in the nest for about four weeks. The young birds soon venture out on their own for short periods of time. But their parents continue to feed them until the babies are more than two months old.

Sea Lamprey
Petromyzon marinus

Length: up to 3 feet
Diet: blood and body fluids of other animals
Number of Eggs: 60,000 to 240,000

Home: North Atlantic and North Pacific oceans
Order: lampreys
Family: lampreys

 Oceans and Shores

 Fish

© BRECK P. KENT / ANIMALS ANIMALS / EARTH SCENES

In many ways, the sea lamprey does not look like a fish. It does not have fins on its sides. It does not have scales. And it does not have jaws. What it does have is a round mouth filled with more than a hundred teeth. The lamprey makes good use of its mouth and teeth. It is a parasite, and it feeds off the blood and body fluids of other fish. Using its round mouth like a suction cup, the lamprey attaches itself to the body of a fish. It uses its teeth and its filelike tongue to scrape away a hole in the fish to get at its blood and other fluids. Once attached, it stays with the fish for days, sometimes killing it. During the first half of this century, sea lampreys invaded the Great Lakes. They killed most of the trout and whitefish that lived there. Ichthyologists (fish experts) eventually developed a poison that killed only young sea lampreys.

Sea lampreys live in the North Atlantic and North Pacific oceans. They migrate to freshwater streams only to spawn. Both males and females use their odd mouths to clear small spaces in the stream floors to house the thousands of eggs. This work is exhausting, and soon after the lampreys die.

The larvae that emerge from the eggs look like tiny white worms. For three to seven years they live in the mud, with only their heads free to filter out food from the water. They slowly grow larger, and when they are between 4 and 8 inches long, they change, or metamorphose, into adults.

Medicinal Leech
Hirudo medicinalis

Length: up to 5 inches (stretched out)
Diet: blood
Method of Reproduction: egg layer

Home: temperate Eurasia
Order: leeches
Family: leeches

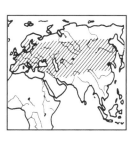

Freshwater

Other Invertebrates

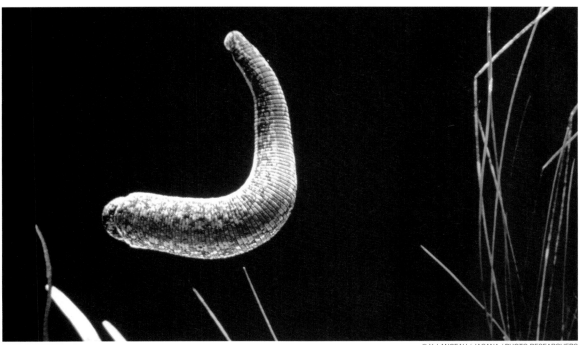

A leech is a type of bloodsucking worm that lives in fresh water. A long time ago, it was thought that a good bloodletting cured all sickness. Doctors and other healers carried leeches with them. They would put leeches on a sick person's body. The leech would suck out blood. The leech attacks frogs, fish, and mammals that enter its territory. It attaches itself to the skin with a sucker that surrounds its mouth. Then it pushes its three little razor-sharp jaws into the flesh. Next it injects chemicals into the victim's body. These chemicals prevent blood from thickening and make blood vessels larger. The leech can drink up to two to five times its own weight of blood. After taking this blood, it lets go of its prey. It drops off into the water to digest its meal for several months. In most parts of the world, medicine no longer uses leeches. However, some doctors still use leeches as a way to remove excess blood from certain kinds of wounds.

The leech swims by waving its body up and down. But it also travels with the help of its two suckers. One of them is near its mouth. There is a more powerful one at the other end of the animal. The leech supports itself first on one sucker, then on the other, curving and stretching its flexible body, moving in a series of horseshoe shapes, like the inchworm.

Brown Lemur
Lemur fulvus

Length of the Body: about 16 inches
Length of the Tail: about 20 inches
Weight: about 6½ pounds
Diet: leaves, grasses, greens, and bark

Number of Young: 1 or 2
Home: Madagascar
Order: primates
Family: true lemurs

Rain Forests

Mammals

© MARTIN HARVEY / PETER ARNOLD, INC.

Endangered
Animals

The Brown lemur has a body like an ape. It has a long, wet nose. It looks like a cross between a monkey and a fox. In fact, lemurs are primitive cousins of monkeys and apes. They are prosimians, or lower primates. Monkeys and apes are called higher primates. Higher primates can make facial expressions. Prosimians cannot. Prosimians are not as intelligent as their higher primate cousins.

Lemurs are rare. That means there are not very many of them left in the world. In Madagascar, people have cut down and destroyed much of the lemur's jungle habitat. Some brown lemurs have learned to live near people and their plantations. But farmers often shoot or poison the animals because they steal and eat valuable crops.

Brown lemurs can also be black, fox red, or any shade in between. They live in the thickest parts of the rain forest. They are adapted for life in the treetops. They can leap between branches 25 feet apart. To hide from flying predatory birds, brown lemurs jump to the ground and run through the jungle underbrush.

Brown lemurs live in peaceful family groups of 6 to 15 animals. They are not territorial and often bed down for the night in groups called tribes. They even share their feeding areas with other lemur species. The entire tribe shows great interest in each new baby.

Ring-tailed Lemur
Lemur catta

Length of the Body: 15 to 20 inches
Length of the Tail: 20 to 25 inches
Weight: 5 to 8 pounds
Diet: fruits, leaves, grasses, and other plant matter

Number of Young: 1
Home: Madagascar
Order: primates
Family: true lemurs

 Forests and Mountains

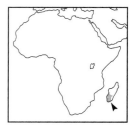

 Mammals

 Endangered Animals

© FRANS LANTING / CORBIS

The ring-tailed lemur is named for the black and white rings on its luxuriously long tail. Some people call this primate the cat lemur because it makes sounds similar to a cat's purr.

Ring-tailed lemurs live in groups of about 20 to 25 members. Within such a group, these animals spend a lot of time grooming one another's fur. Sometimes one ring-tail will even lick another's muzzle to get a taste of what the other lemur has eaten. Each group has its own distinct territory. Members of the group mark tree branches and other objects in the territory with secretions from scent glands on their arms. If another group enters the territory, the home group will attack. They do this to protect both their territory and food supply.

But the main enemies of ring-tailed lemurs are ferret cats and birds of prey.

Wild figs, bananas, and other fruits are the main foods in ring-tailed lemur diets. After eating, these creatures often sunbathe. They find a warm, sunny spot and stretch out with their arms spread wide. Unlike other lemurs, ring-tails spend most of the day on the ground. At night, they rest in trees. All the members of a group sleep in the same tree and often cuddle together to keep warm.

A female ring-tailed lemur is pregnant for about four and a half months before giving birth to one 3-ounce baby. Babies are the center of attention in the group. And everyone enjoys sharing in raising the youngsters.

Leopard
Panthera pardus

Length: 3 to 5 feet
Height at the Shoulder: up to 28 inches
Weight: 65 to 175 pounds
Diet: carnivorous

Number of Young: 2 to 4
Home: Africa and Asia
Order: carnivores
Family: cats

 Forests and Mountains

 Mammals

© FRITZ POLKING / FRANK LANE PICTURE AGENCY / CORBIS

? Endangered Animals

It is dusk. Darkness begins to cover the land. The leopard arises from a nap and begins to hunt. Its long, graceful body moves quietly. It has sharp eyes and an excellent sense of smell. These quickly alert the leopard to the presence of prey. The leopard moves to within striking distance. It then uses its strong back and leg muscles to jump onto the prey. Leopards catch mostly hoofed animals. These include deer and antelope. They also capture baboons, monkeys, rodents, and birds. Leopards that live near farms often snare domesticated animals. They are excellent tree climbers. Sometimes a leopard will pull the remains of its prey up into a tree. This keeps the remains safe from hyenas and other hungry scavengers.

Most leopards live alone. The cubs stay with their mother for the first six months of their lives. How does the mother hunt during that time? She hides the young among rocks or bushes when she goes hunting. She does this for about two months. After that the cubs begin to follow their mother around.

Leopards live in many different habitats. The habitat affects the color of their fur. Leopards in dry, treeless areas usually have pale-colored fur. Forest leopards have dark coats covered with big black spots. Some leopards have black fur. They are called black panthers. Leopards are threatened with extinction for two reasons: People have destroyed their habitats, and they have been hunted for their fur.

Snow Leopard
Uncia uncia

Length: 4 feet
Length of the Tail: 3 feet
Weight: up to 150 pounds
Diet: wild sheep, goats, and other mammals

Number of Young: 2 to 4
Home: Central Asia
Order: carnivores
Family: cats

 Forests and Mountains

 Mammals

© ALAN & SANDY CAREY / ZEFA / CORBIS

? Endangered Animals

Beautiful long fur protects the snow leopard from the freezing temperatures in Central Asia. The fur is thicker in winter than in summer. Unfortunately, the fur also endangers this creature. People trap and kill snow leopards for their luxurious fur. As a result the animal is very scarce and threatened with extinction.

In the wild the snow leopard is seldom seen. This is because it lives in very remote places and hunts only at night. It lives on high, rocky mountains in Central Asia. It migrates with the seasons. During the summer, it prowls in meadows and rocky areas at altitudes up to 19,000 feet above sea level. As winter approaches, it moves down the mountain, staying close to the snow line. The snow leopard rests during the day. Its favorite resting place is in a cave or crevice. Its diet includes wild sheep, wild goats, and deer. It also eats birds and small mammals such as rodents.

Snow leopards are strong and agile. They can leap 10 to 12 feet into the air. And they can clear 30 feet in a single bound. Unlike most cats, snow leopards do not roar. But they make other sounds. For example, they moan loudly to attract mates. Mating occurs in late winter, and the cubs are born in April. The young stay in a warm, cozy den for about two months. Then they begin to go on hunting trips with their mother. They stay close by her side until they are about a year old.

Blue Limpet
Patella caerulea

Length: up to 3 inches
Diet: algae
Method of Reproduction: egg layer
Home: Mediterranean Sea and the Atlantic Ocean around the Canary Islands

Order: button shell mollusks and relatives
Family: true limpets

 Oceans and Shores

 Other Invertebrates

© B. BORRELL CASALS / FRANK LANE PICTURE AGENCY / CORBIS

The pretty blue limpet has a shell that looks like a tiny, pointed lampshade with pleated sides. This limpet's name is somewhat misleading because the outside of its shell is brown or red. The color blue is found only on the inside of its empty shell.

Blue limpets cling to rocks with astonishing strength. Neither the pounding surf nor a curious beachcomber can easily pry this little sea snail off its perch. At high tide, when the limpet is covered with water, it loosens its mighty grip and roams free across the rocks. As it crawls, the limpet looks for algae to eat. It scrapes the algae off the rocks with a rough, tonguelike organ called a radula.

Most blue limpets return home to their special resting places before the water retreats at low tide. Home is typically a small crack or a depression in the rocks. As the tide flows out, the limpet uses strong muscles to pull its shell tight against the rock. In this way, it keeps its soft body from drying out in the open air.

Male and female blue limpets shed tiny clouds of eggs and sperm into the water, where they mix and fertilize. The fertilized eggs hatch into buglike creatures that float through the water. They grow larger and change body shape several times before settling onto the rocks and transforming into adults.

Banded Linsang
Prionodon linsang

Length of the Body: up to 18 inches
Length of the Tail: up to 17 inches
Weight: about 1½ pounds
Diet: small mammals, birds, snakes, insects, and eggs

Number of Young: 2 or 3
Home: Southeast Asia
Order: carnivores
Family: civets, mongooses

 Rain Forests

 Mammals

© TOM MCHUGH / PHOTO RESEARCHERS

The banded linsang is an elegant-looking creature. It is long and slender, with a short, velvety coat. It is a type of viverrid. This is a family of fierce and quick-moving carnivores native to Europe, Asia, and Africa. This linsang looks like a cross between a cat and a weasel. But zoologists chose to name it for the five bands of black spots along its back and the seven black-and-tan rings on its thick, fuzzy tail. Most viverrids have powerful scent glands, which they use to mark their territories. But the banded linsang and its close cousin, the spotted linsang, are uniquely odorless. Both species can retract their claws in a catlike fashion. This trait is not shared by other viverrids.

The banded linsang is a solitary hunter that is active mainly at night. It is a quick and agile climber. And it lives primarily in the trees. However, it also hunts along the rain forest floor. With amazing speed, it can chase down most small animals. Banded linsangs are also fond of eggs, which they crush between their front paws before eating.

The nocturnal linsang is difficult to observe. But naturalists believe the female gives birth twice a year, in May and August. The pregnant female usually makes her nest in a burrow, in a fallen hollow log, or in a hidden place among bushes and weeds. Her young open their eyes when they are 20 days old. They leave their mother at the age of four months.

Lion
Panthera leo

Length: 8 to 10½ feet (male);
   8 to 9 feet (female)
Height: 3 to 4 feet
Weight: 330 to 530 pounds
   (male); 260 to 300 pounds
   (female)

Diet: mammals
Number of Young: 1 to 6
Home: Africa south of the
   Sahara
Order: carnivores
Family: cats

 Grasslands

 Mammals

© FRITZ POLKING / BRUCE COLEMAN INC.

Lions don't do much during the day. They hunt at night. Hunting occurs in mixed groups of males and females. The lions sit quite still, hidden in the grass. The lionesses usually do the actual killing. The males guard them or help move the prey toward the lionesses. The lionesses then jump on the prey and kill it. They bite the nape of the victim's neck or its throat. Lions can eat up to 65 pounds of meat in a single meal. But they don't need to eat every day. Their favorite prey are antelope, zebra, and gazelle. Sometimes they also feed on buffalo or giraffe.

Lions live together in groups called prides. During the night, and especially toward morning, lions show their power by roaring. A lion's roar can be heard for 2 miles. Some think that only the male lion roars. But that is not true. Both sexes roar to communicate. Lions also roar to show ownership of their territory. They mark their territory with urine. Lions mate during the day. A litter is born about three and a half months after mating occurs. A litter usually consists of one to six cubs. The cubs are born blind and usually weigh 3 pounds.

Lions were once found in southern Europe, Asia, and Africa. Today, they live only on savannas south of the Sahara. Lions do not live in tropical forests. So their common nickname, "king of the jungle," is not accurate. The lion's large size and loud roar allow it to live a quiet life. Predators do not disturb this animal.

Armadillo Lizard
Cordylus cataphractus

Length: 8 inches
Weight: 6 to 8 ounces
Diet: grasshoppers, beetles, termites, earthworms, and spiders

Number of Young: 1 to 6
Home: South Africa
Order: scaled reptiles
Family: girdle-tailed lizards

  Deserts

Reptiles

© ROD PATTERSON / GALLO IMAGES / CORBIS

Most lizards are quick and agile. But not the armadillo lizard! This lizard looks like a medieval knight. It carries a coat of heavy armor. Its protective scales look like the hard, plated skin of true armadillos. True armadillos are burrowing mammals found in South America.

Like the true armadillo, an armadillo lizard can curl up to protect its soft belly from the bites of predators. Real armadillos curl into a ball to protect their bellies. The armadllo lizard grasps its sharp tail in its mouth to form a spiky hoop. It can also squeeze its flat body into tight spaces, such as stone crevices. Once this reptile has wedged itself between rocks, predators such as snakes and foxes have a tough time

removing it. If an armadillo lizard is forced to fight, it will lash out with its sharply scaled tail.

Armadillo lizards mate in spring and early summer. Like all reptiles, this species produces eggs. The female keeps the eggs inside her body until they hatch. She gives birth to several live young in late summer or early fall.

Wild armadillo lizards are found only in the granite rock formations that are common in a small area of South Africa. They also make good terrarium pets. They simply require a clean, dry cage. Armadillo lizards tolerate a wide range of temperatures and eat a variety of insects.

Ornate Tree Lizard
Urosaurus ornatus

Length: 4 to 5 inches
Diet: insects and spiders
Number of Eggs: usually 6 to 9
Home: southwestern United States and Mexico

Order: scaled reptiles
Family: North American spiny lizards

 Deserts

Reptiles

© JOE MCDONALD / CORBIS

The ornate tree lizard has the fascinating ability to change color throughout the day. In the cool desert morning, it is dark. This allows it to absorb heat from the sun. As the desert sun gets hotter, the tree lizard's skin grows lighter. Light colors reflect sunlight. This helps the lizard stay cool.

The ornate tree lizard lives in bushes and spiny mesquite trees. These are rust-colored plants. The lizard's dull coloration blends well with them. The tree lizard is very good at playing dead. It will hold perfectly still as a predator approaches. It runs only if it thinks it's been spotted. Then it will quickly disappear down a crack in a tree or a hole in the ground.

Tree lizards are territorial animals. The female spends most of her time in a very specific area of her chosen bush or tree. This is her home range. She will mate only with males who enter it. So a male will establish a territory that overlaps the home range of several females. A trunk or large branch would be a good example. And what if another male should enter that territory? The defender will bob its head up and down. He also shows the bluish green spots of his belly. This usually scares off a weaker male.

Tree lizards mate in late summer. The female lays her eggs in the sand at the base of her home tree. She can lay up to a dozen eggs. But if food is scarce, she will lay only three or four.

Llama
Lama glama

Length: 6 to 7½ feet
Height: 3½ to 4 feet
Weight: 130 to 165 pounds
Diet: grasses, leaves, and bushes
Number of Young: 1

Home: Andes mountains of South America
Order: even-toed hoofed mammals
Family: camels and relatives

 Forests and Mountains

 Mammals

© ROBERT LLEWELLYN / ZEFA / CORBIS

There are four related members of the camel family that live high in the Andes mountains of South America. The llama and alpaca have been tamed for thousands of years. They are no longer found in the wild. The guanaco and vicuña are wild camels. They have never been tamed.

The llama is a good source of food and a great work animal. An adult llama can carry over 150 pounds. It can even travel 18 miles per day carrying that weight. It can go everywhere in the mountains. It can even ascend to elevations of higher than 13,000 feet. Fallen rocks and difficult mountain paths do not stop the llama. Its meat is good to eat. Its hide is used to make sandals and saddles. Its fat is used to make candles. In addition, its droppings are used for fuel. Its bones are used to make sculptures and weapons. And that is not all! The female provides quality wool. But the wool is not as fine as that of the alpaca or the vicuña.

The mating season begins at the end of the summer. It begins with fights between males over the females. The two fighters try to bite each other and to make each other fall. The victor mates with a female llama. Some 11 months later, a single young llama is born.

Llamas had religious importance to the Incas. The Incas were the rulers of the Andes when the Spaniards first came. Llamas were the most precious gift that one could give to the gods.

American Lobster
Homarus americanus

Length: up to 3 feet
Weight: 25 pounds or more
Diet: fish, invertebrates, algae, and eelgrass
Method of reproduction: egg layer

Home: Atlantic Coast of North America
Order: crabs, crayfishes, lobsters, prawns, and shrimp
Family: clawed lobsters

 Oceans and Shores

 Arthropods

© ANDREW J. MARTINEZ / PHOTO RESEARCHERS

The American lobster is greenish black on top and yellowish underneath. This is its color in the water. When cooked, it turns bright red. Many people love to eat American lobsters. And lobster fishing is an important industry in New England. But overfishing has reduced the number of lobsters. Large lobsters are now rare. Most are caught when they are quite young.

An American lobster has five pairs of legs. The first pair is very large. One of the front legs ends in a sharp, pointed claw. This is known as a pincer. It is used to tear apart dead fish. This is the lobster's favorite food. The other front leg has a heavy, blunt pincer with rounded bumps. It is used to crack clamshells and other hard objects. American lobsters live on the ocean bottom. They are usually found in crevices or burrowed under rocks.

A female lobster produces thousands of eggs each year. The eggs are attached to appendages. These are called swimmerets. They are on the lower side of the female's belly. When the eggs hatch, the larvae swim to the surface of the sea. During the next week, fish eat many of the larvae. Those that survive settle at the bottom of the ocean. There they grow into adults and spend the rest of their lives.

Caribbean Spiny Lobster
Panulirus argus

Length: up to 24 inches
Weight: up to 18 pounds
Diet: mollusks and sea cucumbers
Number of Eggs: up to 4 million

Home: Atlantic coast from North Carolina to Brazil
Order: crabs, crayfishes, lobsters, prawns, and shrimp
Family: spiny lobsters

  Oceans and Shores

 Arthropods

© STEPHEN FRINK / CORBIS

Caribbean spiny lobsters live near rocks or reefs in water no more than 300 feet deep. Much like an army, hundreds of these lobsters march along the ocean floor single file. These lines are as long as 60 miles during their seasonal migrations. How can such large groups stay in line? They use their antennae to communicate and to feel where the lobsters ahead of and behind them are going. They also communicate by sound. The lobsters make noises by rubbing their antennae against small ridges near their eyes.

Female Caribbean spiny lobsters lay their eggs between March and July. The eggs hatch one month later. Newly hatched spiny lobsters are called phyllosomes. These leaf-shaped young don't crawl on the ocean bottom like adult lobsters. Instead, they drift through the water like plankton. They are very different from the adults. For many years, scientists didn't realize that phyllosomes and spiny lobsters were the same species.

When they are about seven months old, phyllosomes change their shape to resemble tiny adult spiny lobsters. At this point, they are less than an inch long. They sink to the ocean floor and quickly double in size. They do this by shedding their shells and growing new ones again and again. They continue to shed their shells as they grow about 1 inch per year throughout their lives. Caribbean spiny lobsters are eaten by groupers and other large fish, as well as by humans.

Common Loon
Gavia immer

Length: 2 to 3 feet
Weight: 6 to 14 pounds
Diet: fish
Number of Eggs: 2
Summer Home: Canada and northern United States

Winter Home: Atlantic and Pacific coasts and the Gulf of Mexico
Order: auks, herons, and relatives
Family: loons

 Freshwater

 Birds

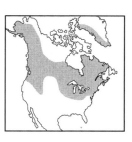

Loons get their name from an old Scandinavian word meaning "oaf." This is probably because they are so clumsy on land. Loons are large aquatic birds with short legs. These legs are almost totally buried in their bodies. This makes walking difficult. But in the water or in the air, these birds are powerful and graceful.

A loon spends most of its time floating in lakes and ponds. It looks for fish swimming just below the surface. When it spots a fish, the loon points its beak into the water and dives. It moves through the water with its feet, using its wings to steer. Loons are also powerful fliers. They take off oddly. They run across the surface of the water and flap their huge wings. But once they are in the air, loons can fly as fast as 75 miles per hour. Loons rarely walk on land. They do so only when they want to mate or when they need to lay and tend their eggs. Their favorite nesting places are on small islands. Both male and female loons take care of the hatchlings. The parents protect their young from being eaten by snapping turtles or large fish. They allow the chicks to ride on their backs for the first two weeks after they leave the nest.

The loon is a very vocal bird. It is best known for its call. This is a long, melodic "ah-oooo-ah." It is followed by what sounds like crazy laughter. This call has led people to use the expression "crazy as a loon."

Canadian Lynx
Lynx canadensis

Length: 2½ to 3 feet
Height: 2 to 2½ feet
Weight: up to 30 pounds
Diet: hares, rabbits, rodents, birds, fish, and deer

Number of Young: 1 to 5
Home: northern North America
Order: carnivores
Family: cats

 Forests and Mountains

 Mammals

? Endangered Animals

© JOE MCDONALD / CORBIS

With its ears perked up and its eyes watchful, it walks silently through the Canadian forest. Its large, hairy front paws and long legs keep it from sinking too deeply into the snow. It has little tufts of hair at the tips of its ears. This is the Canadian lynx. Its vision is piercing. So the expression *lynx-eyed* means to have keen vision.

The Canadian lynx stalks or chases its prey. Then it literally jumps on its victim. Its favorite foods are hare and rabbit. But it also eats small rodents and even some deer. The lynx is a very good swimmer, and it likes to fish. It hunts at night. During the day it rests in the shelter of a fallen tree, a dense shrub, or some rocks. The lynx population increases at the same rate as the number of hares. When the hare population decreases, the number of lynx soon falls.

The Canadian lynx lives in a territory that ranges from 4 to 100 square miles. It lives a solitary life except in mating season. At that time, the female leaves her young, born the year before, to search for a mate. After the breeding season, the female returns to her territory. About three months later, she has from one to five kittens. They open their eyes when they are about 16 days old. When they are a month old, they begin to feed on the meat their mother brings. They stay with her for a year. Lynx are greatly hunted for their beautiful fur. But there are still many of them in the Canadian forest.

Barbary Macaque
Macaca sylvanus

Length: 15 to 30 inches
Weight: 11 to 30 pounds
Diet: fruits, leaves, bark, roots, and invertebrates
Number of Young: 1 to 2

Home: Gibraltar and North Africa
Order: primates
Family: Old World monkeys

 Forests and Mountains

 Mammals

© MARKUS BOTZEK / ZEFA / CORBIS

Barbary macaques are often called Barbary apes. They are the only monkeys that live in the wild in Europe and northwestern Africa. In Europe, they are found only on Gibraltar, a British-governed peninsula in southern Spain. The macaques have lived there for hundreds of years, but no one is sure how they reached Gibraltar. Some people believe they were brought by British soldiers. And there is a superstition that if the macaques disappear from Gibraltar, British rule there will end. Tourists enjoy seeing the macaques, but residents of the peninsula consider them pests. They enter people's gardens and even invade their homes!

The Barbary macaques in Africa live in the forests of the Atlas Mountains. There they enjoy the warm summers and abundant fruits and other good food. Winter is more difficult for these monkeys because it becomes cold and often snows. The macaques grow a thick, warm coat of fur and must eat hard-to-digest foods like leaves and bark instead of their delicious summer diet.

Barbary macaques live in groups of 12 to 40 individuals. The female macaque is pregnant for seven months, and the baby weighs about 1 pound at birth. The animals make good parents. The mother macaque gives her baby lots of care and attention. And others in the group, including males, help care for the young. They carry and groom them and even play with the babies.

Liontail Macaque
Macaca silenus

Length of the Body: up to 24 inches
Length of the Tail: up to 15 inches
Weight: up to 22 pounds
Diet: insects, blossoms, fruits, and nuts

Number of Young: usually 1; rarely twins
Home: southwestern India
Order: primates
Family: Old World monkeys

 Rain Forests

Mammals

© FRANS LANTIN / CORBIS

? Endangered Animals

The liontail macaque could also be called "lion-faced." This is because of its dramatic mane of pale gray hair. The monkey's bright beard contrasts with the dark fur on the rest of its body. The liontail is considered the most striking of the 16 species of macaques. Unfortunately, it may also be the rarest. Local people kill liontails for their beautiful fur and their meat. To make matters worse, logging has destroyed much of the macaque's tropical rain forest home. As a result, there may be fewer than 400 liontails left in the wild today. Another 300 or so live in zoos.

The liontail macaque's best defense against enemies, including humans, is its habit of staying high in the trees, as far as 95 feet above the jungle floor. When this monkey does come to the ground, it is quick to jump back into the branches at the slightest sound of danger. As a troop of liontails moves across the treetops, the leading male often cries out loudly. His call helps gather members of the group together and also alerts other monkeys to the troop's presence.

Female liontails are several pounds lighter and several inches shorter than the males. Young liontail macaques are ready to mate by the time they are four years old. About six months after breeding, the female gives birth. She nurses and cares for her baby for more than a year.

Mallard
Anas platyrhynchos

Length: 20 to 28 inches
Weight: 2½ to 3¼ pounds
Diet: omnivorous
Number of Eggs: 8 to 10
Home: Eurasia, North Africa, and North America

Order: ducks, geese, swans, waterfowl
Family: ducks, geese, and swans

 Freshwater

 Birds

© PHIL KLEIN / CORBIS

The hot June sun blazes down on the small reed-bordered forest pond. Nothing moves. All at once, a shape shoots out of the stillness. It's a mallard duck. It flies almost straight up, noisily and quickly, air hissing in its wings. Then it swoops down and takes refuge on the other side of the pond. There it will spend hours hidden in the reeds.

The mallard is found everywhere in Europe and North America. The male is called a drake. He is known for his green head and neck. A white collar separates his neck from his beautiful brown breast. In flight, a blue bar, called a speculum, decorates his wings. The female is light mottled brown. Her only touches of color are the blue speculum on her wings.

Mallards adore the water. It is where they dabble about and nest. But they come ashore to eat. They graze on prairie grass. They will devour all kinds of seeds. In the water, they are often seen in the vertical position. Their head is probing the mud beneath the surface. The rump and feet stick out above the water. The ducks are looking for seeds. They will also eat small crustaceans, mollusks, and fish.

The female sits on the eggs. She also takes care of the young by herself. The young follow their mother for some days after hatching. Like most ducks, mallards are sociable birds. They join together with other ducks to migrate in the late fall. They travel at night and rest during the day.

Green Mamba
Dendroaspis angusticeps

Length: up to 6½ feet
Diet: mainly lizards and birds
Number of Eggs: 10 to 15
Home: eastern Africa, from
   Kenya south to Zimbabwe

Order: scaled reptiles
Family: cobras, coral snakes

 Rain Forests

 Reptiles

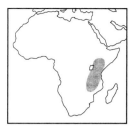

© DANIEL HEUCLIN / BIOS / PETER ARNOLD, INC.

The green mamba spends most of its life in trees. There its leaflike coloration helps it blend in with the jungle background. This creature can move extraordinarily fast for a snake. One green mamba has been clocked speeding along at a remarkable 7 miles per hour. This rate is at least twice that of any North American snake.

Like all mambas, the green variety packs an extremely poisonous venom. But when the green mamba sets out looking for its next meal, it moves about slowly. It holds its head high with its mouth open, exposing fierce-looking fangs. When the prey is within striking range, the mamba attacks. The fangs pierce through the prey, all the while injecting a whitish venom. The venom affects the victim's nervous system, especially the part that controls the heart and breathing.

The green mamba tends to avoid humans. It is, in fact, much less aggressive than other mamba species. Nonetheless, many humans are bitten each year by the green mamba. But this usually happens only if they directly confront or pursue the snake. A person bitten by a green mamba faces a true medical emergency. The green mamba usually strikes at a human's legs or torso. And the venom works very rapidly. The victim must be treated quickly with a special antivenin (a medication that neutralizes the venom). Otherwise, death is almost certain.

Portuguese Man-of-War
Physalia physalia

Length: 40 to 60 feet
Diet: small fish and plankton
Method of Reproduction: asexual
Home: Atlantic, Indian, and Pacific oceans at middle latitudes

Order: bluebottles and relatives
Family: bluebottles

 Oceans and Shores

 Other Invertebrates

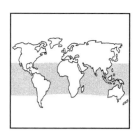

© STUART WESTMORELAND / CORBIS

The Portuguese man-of-war is one of the best known—and most dangerous—of the jellyfish. It looks like a single, elaborate animal. But it is actually a colony of individual organisms that function as one. Within its body, different types of one-celled organisms have special jobs to do. The cells that make up the man-of-war's tentacles are especially dangerous. They form tangles of deadly stingers that hang from the man-of-war's floating, gas-filled bladder. These tentacles may reach lengths of 100 feet!

The Portuguese man-of-war is a fearsome predator. Its stinging tentacles can seriously injure and even kill swimmers who run into them. Even a dead or disabled man-of-war can cause great harm. So if you ever see one washed up on a beach, keep your distance! The gas-filled bladder that helps the man-of-war float is filled with carbon dioxide and oxygen. This bubble acts like a ship's sail. It catches the ocean current instead of the wind. A large group of these fish traveling together through the water resembles an armada of ancient sailing vessels.

Despite the man-of-war's fearsome weapons, some small fish dare to live among its tentacles. These brave fish even break off and eat pieces of their host. However, they are not immune to the man-of-war's sting. A clumsy fish can easily become dinner instead of a guest.

Giant Manta
Manta birostris

Length: up to 24 feet
Width: up to 12 feet
Weight: 1 ton
Diet: plankton, small fish, and crustaceans
Number of Young: 1

Home: Hawaiian Islands and tropical western Pacific Ocean
Order: stingrays
Family: devil rays, mantas

 Oceans and Shores

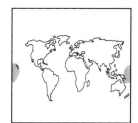

 Fish

© AMOS NACHOUM / CORBIS

This huge, fast ray was given its species name in honor of Prince Alfred. He was the fourth child of Queen Victoria of England. *Manta* comes from the Spanish word for blanket. And these flat, thin fish do, indeed, look like flying blankets.

Giant mantas often travel in groups of two or four individuals. They swim wing tip to wing tip. Standing beneath them, divers would think they were seeing a fleet of underwater stealth bombers. But they are far more graceful. The giant manta has broad triangular "wings." They curl through the water like flying carpets. Sometimes giant mantas race to the surface of the water. They leap into the air. Then they land with a spectacular belly flop and a giant splash.

Mantas are built to eat on the run. The mantas mouth stretches the entire width of its head. It holds its mouth open as it "flies" through the ocean. In this way, it scoops up hundreds of pounds of food. Its eats plankton, crustaceans, and small fish. The manta also has two soft, movable horns, or "head fins." There is one at each corner of its mouth. These help the manta gather its food. The giant manta has little need for teeth. This is because its prey comes in little morsels. It has several rows of very small teeth on its lower jaw. There are no teeth at all on the top of its mouth.

Praying Mantis
Mantis religiosa

Length: 1½ to 3 inches
Diet: insects
Method of Reproduction: egg layer
Home: southern Europe and North America

Order: cockroaches, termites, mantids
Family: mantids and praying mantids

  Grasslands

Arthropods

© TIM DAVIS / CORBIS

The praying mantis is perfectly still in the meadows or in the forest. Its forelegs are raised toward the sky. The mantis seems to be praying. It is actually waiting for its prey to approach. Crickets are the mantis's favorite food. Its forelegs are powerful weapons. They can stretch out in a second to capture an insect. The spines on its legs hold the victim securely and prevent it from escaping.

A mantis may resemble a leaf, flower, stem, or vine, depending on its species. In spite of her large wings, the female is too heavy to fly. Only the male, which is much smaller, can fly. The fate of the male is not always a good one. The female may eat him as soon as they have finished mating.

The female mantis shelters her eggs in an egg case called an ootheca. When she lays her eggs, she produces a sticky substance that she beats into foam. She puts her eggs in this foam, which hardens and protects the eggs. Then, thousands of larvae come out. They are usually quickly eaten by ants and lizards. Only a few of the little mantises escape.

Most mantises live in warm places. Both the eastern American species and the European species like woodlands. They also prefer meadows and sunny areas. Farmers and gardeners often buy egg cases of the Chinese praying mantis, *Tenodera aridifolia*. They hatch them in the hope that they will eat harmful pests.